CW00541005

This edition published by G2 Rights
© copyright 2015 G2 Rights Ltd

ISBN 978-1-909040-05-2

Compiled by Adam Sykes, Iain Sproat and Pat Morgan
Cover drawing by John Ireland

CHAPTER 1

The Wit and Wisdom of Sir Winston

Sir Winston Leonard Spencer Churchill made an unconventional entry to this world. The son of Lord Randolph Churchill and Lady Jennie arrived prematurely in a small room, which was at the time serving as a ladies' cloakroom, at Blenheim Palace, Oxfordshire on the night of 30 November 1874.

After a life marked by frequent similarly unconventional incidents, he died quietly on the morning of 24 January 1965 in a bedroom at 28 Hyde Park Gate, London after a week's coma caused by a stroke.

Between those two dates, Churchill lived a life so extraordinary and made such an indelible mark on the history of the twentieth century that in 2002 the people of the United Kingdom voted him the greatest Briton who ever drew breath.

Sportsman, soldier, orator, statesman, historian, painter, prophet and writer, he was also celebrated – perhaps more than for anything else – for his wit. Sir Robert Menzies, prime minister of Australia, noted as much when he spoke on the occasion of Churchill's funeral: 'Winston was a man of wit and chuckling humour.'

The British prime minister Harold Macmillan agreed. 'Perhaps the most endearing thing about Sir Winston Churchill in private talk, in cabinet, in the House of Commons, was his puckish humour, his tremendous sense of fun and the quick alteration between grave and gay,' he said on the day of Churchill's death.

His wit manifested itself in many ways – puckish, infectious, hilarious, downright rude – but its one constant characteristic was that it could be unveiled anywhere, at any time, in even the gravest conditions.

In this book you will find the best of that wit – ripe plums of humour taken from Churchill's parliamentary replies and ripostes, prepared addresses, asides and off-the-cuff remarks – all revealing a trenchant sharpness of mind, fine appreciation of humour and devastating sense of fun.

Perhaps the most searing examples of his razor-edged wit were directed at his parliamentary adversaries in the cut and thrust of the political scene. When Sir Alfred Bossom made his initial entry into the House of Commons, Churchill was heard to say: 'Bossom? Bossom? What an extraordinary name ... neither one thing nor the other.'

When seriousness was demanded, however, Churchill rose to the occasion like no other orator. His defiant discourses to parliament, the British nation and listeners overseas during World War II have rightly passed into legend as brilliant examples of the speechmaker's art, and a section of this book is given over to print versions of those speeches, so that you may follow – perhaps even commit to memory – the great man's words.

Britain, and the world, have changed irrevocably since 1965, but even in today's brave new world, Churchill's wit and wisdom retain their startling originality and biting power. They are timeless.

CHAPTER 2

Churchill on Churchill

A prolific writer as well as a noted speaker, Churchill offered many an appreciation of his contemporaries – but also of himself.

*

'I am not usually accused, even by my friends, of a modest or retiring disposition.'

*

Churchill became prime minister for the first time in 1940. He later wrote: *'I felt as if I were walking with destiny, and that all my past life had been but a preparation for this hour and for this trial.'*

*

His youth and education were not entirely happy experiences. *'I was what,'* he once recalled, *'people called "a troublesome boy".'*

*

'Where my reason, imagination or interest were not engaged, I would not or I could not learn,' he said of his school days.

*

Later in life, though, he admitted: *'I am always ready to learn, although I do not always like being taught".*

*

"I am certainly not one of those who need to be prodded,' said Churchill. *'In fact, if anything, I am the prod.'*

*

If staff or ministers received a memorandum from WSC bearing the words 'action this day', they knew delay was not an option. *'I never worry about action,'* Churchill was heard to say, *'but only inaction.'*

*

'I am easily satisfied with the very best.'

*

'Although prepared for martyrdom, I preferred that it be postponed,' said Churchill of his early life.

*

Of his wartime stewardship of Britain, he stated: *'I was only the servant of my country and had I, at any moment, failed to express her unflinching resolve to fight and conquer, I should at once have been rightly cast aside.'*

*

'We are all worms. But I do believe I am a glow-worm.'

*

'In the course of my life, I have often had to eat my words, and I must confess that I have always found it a wholesome diet.'

*

'There is no such thing as a negative virtue,' declared Churchill. *'If I have been of service to my fellow man, it has never been by self-repression, but always by self-expression.'*

*

'For myself, I am an optimist. It does not seem to be much use being anything else.'

*

Churchill's marriage to Clementine was a long and happy one, but he insisted: *'My most brilliant achievement was my ability to be able to persuade my wife to marry me.'*

*

'I do think unpunctuality is a vile habit, and all my life I have tried to break myself of it.'

CHAPTER 3

Thoughts and Opinions

It sometimes seemed that you could name any topic, and Churchill had thought about it, and could express an opinion.

*

A visitor once famously remarked on the likeness of one of his grandchildren to Winston, who, equally famously, replied: *'All babies are like me.'*

*

'Politics are almost as exciting as war and quite as dangerous, although in war you can be killed only once, in politics many times.'

*

Hansard of 13 May 1940 reported this Churchillian musing on democracy: *'Many forms of Government have been tried, and will be tried in this world of sin and woe. No one pretends that democracy is perfect or all-wise. Indeed, it has been said that democracy is the worst form of government except all those other forms that have been tried from time to time.'*

*

In another pronouncement on democracy, Churchill remarked: *'The best argument against democracy is a five-minute conversation with the average voter.'*

*

'Some men change their party for the sake of their principles; others their principles for the sake of their party.'

*

'When the eagles are silent, the parrots begin to jabber.'

*

Paris in the years immediately following World War I was described by Churchill as *'a terrible society, grimly polished and trellised with live wires.'*

*

'The press is easier squashed than squared.'

*

Churchill once described Europe between the two world wars thus: *'Dictators ride to and fro upon tigers which they dare not dismount. And the tigers are getting hungry.'*

*

Why, Winston was once asked, did he always seem to miss trains and aeroplane flights? *'I am a sporting man,'* he replied. *'I always give them a fair chance of getting away.'*

*

'A joke is a very serious thing.'

*

'Trying to maintain good relations with the communists is like wooing a crocodile. You do not know whether to tickle it under the chin or beat it over the head. When it opens its mouth you cannot tell whether it is trying to smile or preparing to eat you up.'

*

*'I like pigs. Dogs look up to us. Cats look down on us.
Pigs treat us as equals.'*

*

*'A fanatic is one who can't change his mind and won't
change the subject.'*

*

When Churchill was in his seventy-sixth year, he
was asked if he had any fear of death. His reply was
quiet and considered: *'I am ready to meet my maker.
Whether my maker is prepared for the great ordeal
of meeting me is another matter.'*

*

'Would you like to tell our readers, sir,' a journalist
once asked, 'what are the desirable qualifications
for any young man who wishes to be a politician?
'Churchill's face took on its well-known 'bulldog
look', and all those present assumed he was about
to come out with a profound nugget of wisdom. *'It
is the ability,'* he rumbled thoughtfully, *'to foretell
what is going to happen tomorrow, next week,
next month and next year.'* He stopped and glanced
round the assembled journalists to make sure they
had got all that down, and then added: *'And to*

have the ability afterwards to explain why it didn't happen.'

*

'There is no finer investment for any community than putting milk into babies.'

*

Churchill was not sure of the benefits of some examples of twentieth century technology, and sometimes regretted the passing of equine power. *'I have always considered that the substitution of the internal combustion engine for the horse,'* he remarked, *'marked a very gloomy milestone in the progress of mankind.'*

*

'Broadly speaking,' Churchill declared, *'human beings may be divided into three classes: those who are billed to death; those who are worried to death; and those who are bored to death.'*

*

'Don't argue about the difficulties. The difficulties will argue for themselves.'

*

Churchill might not always be perceived as having been receptive to criticism, but he stated: *'Criticism may not be agreeable, but it is necessary. It fulfils the same function as pain in the human body; it calls attention to the development of an unhealthy state of things. A young man cannot expect to get very far in life without getting some good smacks in the eye.'*

*

Churchill was loath to make prophecies. *'It is a mistake to look too far ahead,'* he said. *'Only one link of the chain of destiny can be handled at a time.'*

*

On another occasion, he remarked: *'It is always wise to look ahead, but difficult to look further than you can see.'*

*

At a London meeting of the United Europe movement in 1947, Churchill proclaimed: *'All the greatest things are simple, and many can be expressed in a single word: freedom, justice, honour, duty, mercy, hope.'*

*

In 1948 he added these words to the debate on the unity of Europe: *'We are asking the nations of Europe between whom rivers of blood have flowed to forget the feuds of a thousand years.'*

*

'Difficulties mastered are opportunities won.'

*

Churchill was well qualified to judge the courage of others, and did not hesitate to pronounce: *'Courage is rightly esteemed the first of human qualities ... because it is the quality which guarantees all others.'*

*

On another occasion, he observed: *'Courage is what it takes to stand up and speak; courage is also what it takes to sit down and listen.'*

*

'Healthy citizens are the greatest asset any country can have.'

*

'If the human race wishes to have a prolonged and indefinite period of material prosperity, they have only

got to behave in a peaceful and helpful way toward one another.'

*

'If you are going through hell, keep going.'

*

'If you have an important point to make, don't try to be subtle or clever,' advised Churchill. *'Use a piledriver. Hit the point once. Then come back and hit it again. Then hit it a third time – a tremendous whack.'*

*

'It is a fine thing to be honest, but it is also very important to be right.'

*

'Never hold discussions with the monkey when the organ grinder is in the room.'

*

'Nothing can be more abhorrent to democracy than to imprison a person or keep him in prison because he is unpopular. This is really the test of civilisation.'

*

'Perhaps it is better to be irresponsible and right, than to be responsible and wrong.'

*

At school, the young Churchill was often unhappy, and equally often unsuccessful. He found mathematics particularly difficult. He complained: *'The figures were tied in all sorts of tangles and did things to one another which it was extremely difficult to forecast.'*

*

'Play the game for more than you can afford to lose ... only then will you learn the game.'

*

Churchill laid out his hopes for the prosperity and well-being of humankind in a speech in Dundee as early as 1908: *'What is the use of living, if it be not to strive for noble causes and to make this muddled world a better place for those who will live in it after we are gone? How else can we put ourselves in harmonious relation with the great verities and consolations of the infinite and the eternal? And I avow my faith that we are marching towards better days. Humanity will not be cast down. We are going on swinging bravely forward along the grand high road and already behind the distant mountains is the promise of the sun.'*

*

'Solitary trees, if they grow at all, grow strong.'

*

'Some people regard private enterprise as a predatory tiger to be shot,' commented the great man. *'Others look on it as a cow they can milk. Not enough people see it as a healthy horse, pulling a sturdy wagon.'*

*

Never one to hold back an opinion, Churchill was a master of the one-liner:

*

'Success consists of going from failure to failure without loss of enthusiasm.'

*

'Sure I am of this, that you have only to endure to conquer. You have only to persevere to save yourselves.'

*

'The empires of the future are the empires of the mind.'

*

'The longer you can look back, the farther you can look forward.'

*

'The first quality that is needed is audacity.'

*

'The power of man has grown in every sphere, except over himself.'

*

'The price of greatness is responsibility.'

*

'There are a terrible lot of lies going about the world, and the worst of it is that half of them are true.'

*

'There is no such thing as a good tax.'

*

'There is no such thing as public opinion. There is only published opinion.'

*

'To build may have to be the slow and laborious task of years. To destroy can be the thoughtless act of a single day.'

*

'Too often the strong, silent man is silent only because he does not know what to say, and is reputed strong only because he has remained silent.'

*

'We are masters of the unsaid words, but slaves of those we let slip out.'

CHAPTER 4
Other People ...

Hell is other people, thought Jean-Paul Sartre. Sometimes Churchill would have agreed; at other times, not.

*

Churchill once said of David Lloyd George – the only UK prime minister to have spoken English as a second language – that he could *'talk a bird out of a tree'.*

*

Joseph Chamberlain, one of the most influential British politicians of the late nineteenth and early twentieth century, was the subject of this Churchillian observation: *'[He] likes the working classes; he likes to watch them work.'*

*

Churchill once remarked of Joseph Chamberlain's son Neville, prime minister from 1937 to 1940, that he *'looked at foreign affairs through the wrong end of a municipal drainpipe'.*

*

Of three-time prime minister Stanley Baldwin, Churchill observed: *'Occasionally he stumbled over the truth, but hastily picked himself up and hurried on as if nothing had happened.'*

*

He had the highest opinion of statesman and lawyer FE Smith's debating skill: *'The bludgeon for the platform; the entangling net and unexpected trident for the courts of law; and a jug of clear spring water for an anxious, perplexed conclave.'*

*

At a dinner, Churchill was sitting next to Labour politician Sir Stafford Cripps, a strict vegetarian (for health reasons) in an age when choosing not to eat meat was not common. Churchill leant over to his hostess and, glancing mischievously at Cripps, said: *'I am glad I am not a herbivore. I eat what I like, I drink what I like, I do what I like ... and he's the one to have a red nose.'*

*

The much-decorated soldier Field Marshal Bernard Montgomery, known to one and all as Monty, once remarked to Churchill that Lord Longford should have his hair cut. Churchill retorted: *'Your head, my dear Field Marshal, needs to be compressed under a military cap. He needs his for speaking in the House of Lords.'*

*

There was always slight acrimony, at times not without its humour, between Churchill and Bonar Law, the Conservative politician who rose to become prime minister – albeit briefly – in 1922. In a letter, Churchill wrote: *'The words which you now tell me you employed and which purport to be a paraphrase, if not an actual quotation, are separated by a small degree of inaccuracy and misrepresentation from the inaccuracy and misrepresentation of the condensed report.'*

*

On another occasion, he wrote: *'You dance like a will o' the wisp, so nimbly from one unstable foothold to another that my plodding paces can scarcely follow you.'*

*

And: *'I resist all temptation to say, "I told you so"!'*

*

Once again, Churchill was obliged to sit near the austere and gloomy Sir Stafford Cripps at a dinner party. He turned to his neighbour and said: *'Who will relieve me of this wuthering height?'*

*

Churchill once described General Charles de Gaulle, leader of the Free French Forces in London during World War II, in the following memorable way: *'He looks like a female llama who has been surprised in the bath.'*

*

Churchill reserved one of his harsher strictures for Ramsay MacDonald, who became Britain's first Labour prime minister in 1924. *'I remember when I was a child being taken to the celebrated Barnum's circus,'* he recalled. *'The exhibit which I most desired to see was the one described as the "Boneless Wonder". My parents judged that the spectacle would be too revolting and demoralising for my youthful eyes. I have waited fifty years to see the Boneless Wonder sitting on the Treasury bench.'*

*

Of MacDonald he also said, just as memorably: *'He is a sheep in sheep's clothing.'*

*

And, again of the same man: *'We know that he has, more than any other man, the gift of compressing the largest number of words into the smallest amount of thought.'*

*

Churchill once reflected on his relationship with the newspaper magnate Lord Beaverbrook: *'Max is a foul-weather friend.'*

*

At a Council of Europe meeting in Strasbourg in 1950, Churchill found himself sitting one seat away from Dr Hugh Dalton, who had previously been the Labour chancellor of the exchequer. **'I see that we are divided by only one Italian,'** observed Dalton. *'That's not all that divides us,'* grunted Churchill.

*

Sir Stafford Cripps was always a favourite target for Churchill, who saw the Labour politician as all brain and little humanity. One typical attack in a 1946 speech ran: *'Neither of his colleagues can compare with him in that acuteness or energy of mind with which he devotes himself to many topics injurious to the strength and welfare of the state.'*

*

The Liberal politician Charles Masterman professed a great admiration for Keir Hardie, the Scottish labour leader who became one of the founding fathers of the Labour Party. **'He is not a great politician but he will be in heaven before either you or me, Winston,'** said Masterman. Churchill's reply was cutting: *'If heaven is going to be full of people like Hardie, well, the Almighty can have them to himself.'*

*

Back to Sir Stafford Cripps. Churchill spied him walking through the Commons smoking room and remarked: *'There but for the grace of God goes God.'*

*

Churchill once wrote of Sir William Joynson Hicks: *'The worst that can be said about him is that he runs the risk of being humorous when he wishes to be most serious.'*

*

One of Churchill's most famous judgements of his fellow man concerned Labour prime minister Clement

Attlee. *'Mr Attlee is a very modest man,'* he conceded. *'But then he has much to be modest about.'*

*

Of Attlee he also said: *'There is less there than meets the eye.'*

*

Another target of Churchill's was Lord Rosebery, whom he made secretary of state for Scotland in his caretaker administration of 1945. *'It might be said that Lord Rosebery outlived his future by ten years and his past by more than twenty,'* opined Winston.

*

Churchill was fond of making comments about the Labour MP for Ebbw Vale, Aneurin Bevan, and would drag them into his speeches on even the most unlikely occasions. One of these came when he was speaking on the recognition of communist China. *'As we had great interests there [China], and also on general terms, I thought that it would be a good thing to have diplomatic representation,'* said Winston. *'But if you recognise anyone it does not mean that you like him. We all, for instance, recognise the right honourable gentleman the member for Ebbw Vale.'*

*

Churchill strongly criticised Sir Samuel Hoare over the Government of India Bill of 1935 which, when enacted, provided the last constitution of India before its independence. *'The secretary of state [for India] is like a cow who has given a good pail of milk,'* declared Winston, *'but has then kicked it over.'*

*

When the Democrat Al Smith was running for the presidency of the United States in 1928, Churchill suggested that he use *'All for Al, Al for all'* as a slogan.

*

'The difference between [Arthur] Balfour and [Herbert] Asquith is that Arthur is wicked and moral, Asquith is good and immoral.'

*

Churchill: *'I am all for the social order.'*
Lloyd George: **'No! I am against it.'**
Churchill: *'You are not against the social order but only those parts of it which get in your way.'*

*

Of King Farouk, the penultimate king of Egypt and Sudan, Churchill said he was *'wallowing like a sow in a trough of luxury.'*

*

A visitor once asked Edward Marsh, who for more than thirty years was Winston's secretary, what his politics were. Churchill quickly answered for Marsh: *'He is a good Winstonian, of course.'*

*

Sir Stafford Cripps was in the firing line once again when Churchill had enjoyed a very satisfying lunch. *'It is perhaps as well that I was not accompanied by my colleague, the minister of aircraft production [Cripps],'* commented Winston, *'for there is a man who habitually takes his meal off a handful of peas, and, when he gets a handful of beans, counts them his Christmas feast.'*

*

Finally, Churchill is said to have remarked of the unfortunate Cripps: *'He has all of the virtues I dislike and none of the vices I admire.'*

*

Franklin Delano Roosevelt died on 12 April 1945. On a visit to FDR's grave in Hyde Park, New York, Churchill remarked of the great man: *'Meeting Franklin Roosevelt was like opening your first bottle of champagne; knowing him was like drinking it.'*

*

'You can always count on Americans to do the right thing – after they've tried everything else.'

*

Arthur Balfour, prime minister from 1902 to 1905, came in for typically witty Churchill treatment: *'if you wanted nothing done at all, Balfour was the man for the job.'*

*

Churchill's comments on his fellow man could range from subtle wit to savage abuse, as the following examples show.

*

When his forces attacked Greece in October 1940, Italian duce Benito Mussolini was forced to ask his ally Hitler for more troops. Churchill abused him thus: *'Here surely is the world's record in the domain of the ridiculous and the contemptible. This whipped jackal, Mussolini, who to save his own skin has made all Italy a vassal state of Hitler's empire, comes frisking up to the side of the German tiger with yelpings, not only of appetite – that could be understood – but even of triumph.'*

*

In 1941 Hitler's Germany attacked the Soviet Union in Operation Barbarossa. Churchill commented: *'I see advancing in hideous onslaught the Nazi war machine, with its clanking, heel-clicking, dandified Prussian officers, its crafty expert agents fresh from the cowing and tying down of a dozen countries. I see also the dull, drilled, docile, brutish masses of the Hun soldiery plodding on like a swarm of crawling locusts ... they have, of course, the consolation of knowing that they are being led not by the German general staff but by corporal Hitler himself.'*

*

'Into that void strode a maniac of ferocious genius, the expression of the most virulent hatred that has ever corroded the human breast ... corporal Hitler.'

CHAPTER 5

In the House of Commons

The famous debating chamber was the scene of many a memorable Churchill remark, speech or witty riposte.

*

On Churchill's seventy-seventh birthday, a question was raised in the House of Commons designed to show that he was spending valuable dollars on direct importation of cigars. *'I have not for quite a long time imported any cigars from hard-currency areas,'* he told MPs in a formal tone; and then added with a grin: *'I have nevertheless received some from time to time.'*

*

One woman MP, reputed by some to be Labour's Bessie Braddock, once turned on Churchill. *'Mr Churchill, you're drunk, and what's more you're disgustingly drunk,'* she scoffed. *'Bessie, my dear,'* replied Churchill, *'you are ugly, and what's more, you are disgustingly ugly. But tomorrow I shall be sober and you will still be disgustingly ugly.'*

*

'When I am abroad, I always make it a rule never to criticise or attack the government of my own country. I make up for lost time when I come home.'

*

An MP once asked Churchill, then prime minister, if, in view of the current international situation, he would reconsider taking the initiative in an effort to arrange a meeting at top level, representing the USA, the USSR and Britain, in an attempt to lessen the tension. The prime minister replied: *'Perhaps on this somewhat delicate topic I may be permitted by the house to take refuge in metaphor. Many anxieties have been expressed recently at the severe character of the course of the Grand National steeplechase, but I am sure that it could not be improved by asking the horses to try to jump two fences at the same time.'*

*

Clement Attlee, leader of the opposition in 1951, once made a bitter attack on Churchill that was applauded loudly by all sections of the Labour party. Rising to his feet in the Commons, Churchill said: *'A great deal of his speech was made up of very effective points and quips which gave a great deal of satisfaction to those behind him. We all understand his position: "I am their leader, I must follow them."'*

*

In 1948 Churchill defended the death penalty – and specifically hanging – in the House of Commons on the grounds that under English law, if properly conducted, it resulted in an absolutely painless death. This was too much for one MP, who interjected: **'Try it!'** *'Well, it may come to that,'* observed Churchill.

*

On one occasion in 1952, Churchill was accused by the Labour opposition in the Commons of diametrically altering his views. His retort was: *'My views are a harmonious process which keeps them in relation to the current movement of events.'*

*

Hector Hughes, the Labour member for Aberdeen North, once asked the prime minister whether he would reconsider his refusal to separate the Ministry of Agriculture from the Ministry of Fisheries in view of the national importance of the fishing industry; and if he would now take steps to set up a separate ministry to solve its problems and attend to its development.

Food and its production were subjects close to Churchill's heart. *'It would not, I feel, be a good arrangement to have a separate department for every industry of national importance,'* he began.

t*'These two industries have for long been associated departmentally and, after all, there are many ancient links between fish and chips.'*

*

Jean Mann, Labour MP for Coatbridge, pointed out a problem for Scots who regard the current monarch as the first Queen Elizabeth. **'Is the prime minister aware,'** she asked, **'that ... the Mint has decided to issue the coins with "Elizabeth II", and Scots who object to this title are placed in an awful dilemma?'** The prime minister was unsympathetic. *'I hope that theoretical refinements will not stop the normal conduct of business,"* he returned.

*

Dreadful weather during the winter of 1946/47 meant that coal supplies – already low following the war –

often failed to get through to power stations, and the government imposed measures to limit energy consumption. Public morale dipped, and many people blamed Emanuel Shinwell, the Labour government's fuel and power minister.

As industry suffered and controversy raged, Winston, leader of the opposition, was sitting one day in the House of Commons smoking room chatting to friends when up came a tall, austere-looking man. This was Wilson Harris, editor of the Spectator magazine as well as independent MP for Cambridge University. Looming over Sir Winston, the journalist excitedly told him that **'the greatest intellectual weekly in Britain'** – here, his colleague Lord Eccles recalled, Winston was seen to scowl – **'cannot come out for two weeks owing to Mr Shinwell's fuel crisis.'**

Sir Winston was clearly annoyed. In a voice that his friends recognised as meaning trouble, he asked: *'What do you say is going to happen because of Shinwell?'* Harris repeated his claim that the minister must be held responsible for the power cuts, ending up, **'and the Spectator, after a hundred years of continuous publication, will not appear next week or the next.'**

Churchill's scowl melted into a grin. *'I am so glad,'* he purred, and waved Wilson away with his cigar.

*

During the General Strike of 1926, Churchill was made editor of the government-sponsored newspaper the British Gazette. It was the only newspaper published at the time and its aggressive anti-striker tone made it an object of hatred among those sympathetic to the strike.

It was some months after the end of the strike that Churchill suddenly paused in the middle of a violent Commons speech and glared fiercely at the Labour benches.

'I warn you,' he began, and the Commons hushed in expectation of some terrible horror that he was about to unleash, *'I warn you that if ever there is another general strike … we will let loose on you another British Gazette.'*

*

Sir William Joynson Hicks, who was home secretary from 1924 to 1929, was at one time delivering a speech in the House of Commons. He saw Churchill making gestures of disagreement with his theme.

"I see my right honourable friend shakes his head,' said the man nicknamed Jix, **'but I am only**

expressing my own opinion.' *'And I,'* answered Winston, *'am only shaking my own head.'*

*

In 1943, the House of Commons was discussing the rebuilding of the Commons chamber, which had been destroyed by German bombing in 1941. Churchill made this contribution: *'We shape our buildings, and afterwards our buildings shape us.'*

*

In October 1950, the new Commons chamber was opened. A few days before the opening ceremony, Churchill walked into the inner lobby for a quick preview. As he entered, the fluorescent lighting – at that time still something of a novelty – was turned on and Churchill blinked in the harsh white light. *'Good heavens,'* he gasped, *'the Moscow Underground!'*

*

On one occasion in the Commons, something Churchill said caused another member to jump to his feet, expressing his disagreement so excitedly and vociferously that he became almost unintelligible. *'My right honourable friend,'* observed Winston drily, *'should not develop more indignation than he can contain.'*

*

Sir Alan Herbert, the humorist, writer and law reform campaigner, was elected to parliament as an independent member for Oxford University in 1935. His first contribution to Commons debate – termed a maiden speech in parliamentary lingo – was notable for its controversial nature, contrary to custom. Churchill, asked for a comment, exclaimed: *'Call that a maiden speech? It was a brazen hussy of a speech. Never did such a painted lady of a speech parade itself before a modest parliament!'*

*

After a certain statesman had made a speech about the League of Nations in the House of Commons between the two world wars, Churchill was asked for his opinion of it. *'Well,'* he said, *'I thought it was very good. It must have been good; for it contained, so far as I know, all the platitudes known to the human race, with the possible exception of "Prepare to meet thy God" and "Please adjust your dress before leaving".'*

*

Not long after the end of World War II, prime minister Clement Attlee's government proposed to introduce so much legislation that some MPs were feeling the pressure of work. By the time August was approaching, many Members were pressing Herbert Morrison, the deputy prime minister, to say when the parliamentary recess would begin. Churchill rose gravely to his feet. *'We are all anxious for the Labour members to get away in time for the grouse-shooting,'* he informed the house.

*

Churchill once answered a question from Labour politician Aneurin Bevan, instigator of the National Health Service: *'I should think it hardly possible to state the opposite of the truth with more precision.'*

*

A Labour member once asked: **"Is the prime minister aware of the deep concern felt by the people of this country at the whole question of the Korean conflict?"** Churchill replied: *'I am fully aware of the deep concern felt by the honourable member in many matters above his comprehension.'*

*

Another Labour member, Harold Davies (Leek), demanded to know: **'Does the right honourable gentleman realise that the house is getting less information of the Korean situation than his equally great predecessor Mr Gladstone was**

giving the house in the time of the Crimean War?' The prime minister's reply was succinct: *'I am afraid I have not at my fingers' ends the exact part which Mr Gladstone took in the Crimean War; it was even before my time.'*

CHAPTER 6

Britain at War

Churchill was famous for his stirring major wartime speeches as prime minister, but during World War II there were plenty of other opportunities for his wit and wordplay to flourish.

*

A BBC broadcast of 1 October 1939, a month after the start of World War II, contained a comment about the Soviet Union that would soon become well known: *'I cannot forecast to you the action of Russia. It is a riddle wrapped in a mystery inside an enigma: but perhaps there is a key. That key is Russian national interest.'*

*

A wartime memorandum from Churchill to General Sir Hastings Ismay, his trusted chief military advisor, complained of a delay in the manufacture of a new kind of bomb: *'Any chortling by officials who have been slothful in pushing this bomb will be viewed with great disfavour by me.'*

*

During his birthday speech in 1954, Churchill looked back modestly on his role as prime minister throughout World War II: *'I have never accepted what many people have kindly said, namely that I inspired the nation.*

Their will was resolute and remorseless, and as it proved, unconquerable ...

It was the nation and the race dwelling all round the globe that had the lion's heart. I had the luck to be called upon to give the roar.'

*

'I have not become the king's first minister in order to preside over the liquidation of the British Empire.'

*

Churchill sent a wartime memorandum to the minister of food on the question of whether the manufacture of ice cream should be prohibited.

'I cannot judge whether the destruction of this amenity is worth while,' he wrote.

'I suppose the large numbers of American troops in this country will have their own arrangements made for them. They are great addicts of ice cream, which is said to be a rival to alcoholic drinks.'

*

There was another memorandum to the minister of agriculture: *'Have you done justice to rabbit production? Although rabbits are not by themselves nourishing, they are a pretty good mitigation of vegetarianism. They eat mainly grass and greenstuffs, so what is the harm in encouraging their multiplication in captivity?'*

*

During World War II there were complaints about unequal chances of promotion in the navy, and Churchill agreed with them: *'If a telegraphist may rise, why not a painter? Apparently there is no such difficulty about painters rising in Germany ...'*

*

On 29 October 1941, Churchill visited one of his old schools, Harrow, and urged the boys: *'Never give in, never give in, never, never, never, never, in nothing, great or small, large or petty, never give in except to convictions of honour and good sense. Never yield to force; never yield to the apparently overwhelming might of the enemy.'*

*

Perhaps Churchill's finest hour came when he proclaimed: *'We shall fight on the beaches, we shall fight on the landing grounds, we shall fight in the fields and in the streets, we shall fight in the hills; we shall never surrender.'* What is less well known is that, after this famous stirring call to arms, he covered up the microphone with his hand and said: *'And if we can't do that we'll hit them on the head with bottles.'*

*

When Churchill learned that 'communal feeding centres' were to be established in wartime Britain, he sent a strong protest to the minister of food: *'It is an odious expression, suggestive of communism and the workhouse. I suggest that you call them British Restaurants. Everyone associates the word "restaurants" with a good meal, and they may as well have the name if they cannot have anything else.'*

*

Humour was often present in the midst of Churchill's most sombre wartime speeches, and it always went down well with his audiences. Such a moment came during one of his broadcasts to France in 1940: *'We are waiting for the long-promised invasion. So are the fishes.'*

*

On the German invasion of the Soviet Union in 1941: *'There is a winter, you know, in Russia. Hitler forgot about this. He must have been very loosely educated. We all heard about it at school, but he forgot it. I have never made such a bad mistake as that.'*

*

In February 1945, the Yalta conference brought together the 'Big Three' – Churchill, president Franklin D Roosevelt of the USA and general secretary Joseph Stalin of the Soviet Union – to discuss the post-war reorganisation of Europe. Churchill commented: *'I don't see any way of realising our hopes of world organisation in six days. Even the Almighty took seven.'*

*

In May 1941, Rudolf Hess, Hitler's deputy, parachuted into Scotland with the intention of meeting the Duke of Hamilton. The latter promptly sent Churchill a message saying that Hess had arrived in Britain to negotiate a settlement. The prime minister replied: *'Will you kindly instruct the Duke of Hamilton to tell that to the Marx Brothers.'*

*

Later in 1941, General Maitland 'Jumbo' Wilson made a bold attempt to hold the Greek island of Leros with hopelessly insufficient troops. Churchill commented: *'I sent him a signal "improvise and dare", so he improvose and dore.'*

*

At a chiefs of staff meeting in 1941, one of those present advocated that Britain adopt towards the USA the same cautious approach that she had adopted when America's intervention had still seemed in doubt. Churchill disagreed, saying with a wicked gleam in his eye: *'Oh, that is the way we talked to her while we were wooing her; now that she is in the harem, we talk to her quite differently.'*

*

Churchill to Brendan Bracken MP, his ally and confidant: *'You know, you have got to hand it to Hitler. The war has been on only a few minutes and here is an air raid already.'*

*

On the possible German occupation of London: *'If they come to London I shall take a rifle – I'm not a bad shot – I will put myself in a pillbox at the bottom of Downing Street, and shoot till I have no more ammunition, and then they can damn well shoot me.'*

*

'If Hitler invaded hell I would make at least a favourable reference to the devil in the House of Commons.'

*

On the Battle of Egypt in 1942: *'This is not the end, it is not even the beginning of the end. It is perhaps the end of the beginning.'*

*

Referring to the American desire to sack king Victor Emmanuel III of Italy and his prime minister, Pietro Badoglio, in 1944, Churchill said: *'Why break the handle of the coffee pot at this stage and burn your fingers trying to hold it? Why not wait till we get to Rome and let it cool off?'*

*

On the attempt to establish the Anzio bridgehead during the Allied invasion of Italy, Churchill said: *'We hoped to land a wildcat that would tear out the bowels of the Boche. Instead we have stranded a vast whale with its tail flopping about in the water.'*

*

When the war ended, Churchill was surprised to see how little affected those countries under Nazi tyranny had been. He remarked during a drive through France: *'We are surrounded by fat cattle lying in luscious pastures with their paws crossed.'*

*

He had warned those countries that tried to take refuge from Hitler in neutrality: *'Each one hopes that if he feeds the crocodile enough, the crocodile will eat him last.'*

*

Churchill described what Britain's attitude towards Turkey should be in 1943: *'We must start by treating them purry-purry, puss-puss, then later we shall harden!'*

*

General 'Pug' Ismay, Churchill's wartime chief of staff, recalled one late-night discussion by the defence committee on the exact timing of the D-Day landings:

'I regret to admit that I was half asleep when I heard the prime minister ask when William the Conqueror had landed. Hitherto I had made no contribution to the debate. Here was my chance. "1066!" I exclaimed.

'To my surprise this was greeted with a roar of laughter, and the prime minister said pityingly: *"Pug, you should have been in your basket ages ago."'*

*

'Before Alamein we never had a victory. After Alamein we never had a defeat.'

*

Churchill once explained how he had answered the French generals who had asked him how Britain would be able to withstand an invasion.

'So I said that of course I was not a military expert and I was always very careful in not meddling in these sorts of questions, but that my professional advisers told me that the best way to deal with such an invasion would be to drown as many as possible on

*the way over, and knock the rest on the head as they
crawled ashore.'*

*

*'These are not dark days: these are great days – the
greatest days our country has ever lived.'*

*

Churchill's humorous use of understatement was
well known. Of the 1941 Japanese attack on Pearl
Harbour which led to the USA entering World War
II, he told the US Congress: *'They have certainly
embarked upon a very considerable undertaking.'*

*

'The British nation is unique in this respect,' Churchill
said to the Commons in 1941. *'They are the only
people who like to be told how bad things are, who like
to be told the worst, and like to be told that they are
very likely to get much worse in the future and must
prepare themselves for further reverses.'*

CHAPTER 7

The War Speeches

Sir Winston Churchill is probably best remembered for the brilliant speeches of defiance and hope with which he stirred the hearts of his listeners during World War II.

In this chapter you can read the transcripts of speeches from before a shot was fired, from the darkest days of the war and from after the cessation of hostilities, together with others that show just as clearly the Churchillian genius for oratory.

Britain Must Arm, America Must Arm

On 16 October 1938, Churchill broadcast to the United Kingdom and the United States.

Alexander the Great remarked that the peoples of Asia were slaves because they had not learned to pronounce the word 'no'. Let that not be the epitaph of the English-speaking peoples or of parliamentary democracy, or of France, or of the many surviving liberal states of Europe.

There, in one single word, is the resolve which the forces of freedom and progress, of tolerance and goodwill, should take. It is not in the power of one nation, however formidably armed; still less is it in the power of a small group of men – violent, ruthless men, who have always however to cast their eyes back over their shoulders – it is not in their power to cramp and fetter the forward march of human destiny.

The preponderant world forces are upon our side; they have but to be combined to be obeyed. We must arm. Britain must arm. America must arm.

We shall, no doubt, arm. Britain, casting away the habits of centuries, will decree national service for her citizens. But arms – instrumentalities, as president Wilson called them – are not sufficient by themselves. We must add to them the power of ideas.

People say we ought not to allow ourselves to be drawn into a theoretical antagonism between Nazidom and democracy. But the antagonism is here, now.

You see these dictators on their pedestals, surrounded by the bayonets of their soldiers and the truncheons of their police. They are afraid of words and thoughts; words spoken abroad, thoughts stirring at home – all the more powerful because forbidden – terrify them. A little mouse of thought appears in the room, and even the mightiest potentates are thrown into panic. They make frantic efforts to bar our thoughts and words; they are afraid of the workings of the human mind.

A state of society where men may not speak their minds, where children denounce their parents to the police, where a businessman or small shopkeeper ruins his competitor by telling tales about his private opinions; such a state of society cannot long endure if it is brought continually in contact with the healthy outside world.

The light of civilised progress with its tolerances and co-operation, with its dignities and joys, has often been blotted out. But I hold the belief that we have now at last got far enough ahead of barbarism to control it, and to avert it, if only we realise what is afoot and make up our minds in good time.

Is this a call to war? Does anyone pretend that preparation for resistance against aggression amounts to the unleashing of war? I declare it to be the sole guarantee of peace, the finest and the surest prospect of peace.

The Causes of War

Four years before his call to arms, on 16 November 1934, Churchill had warned of the threat posed by Germany under the Nazis.

Many people think that the best way to escape war is to dwell upon its horrors and to imprint them vividly upon the minds of the younger generation. They flaunt the grisly photograph before their eyes. They fill their ears with tales of carnage. They dilate upon the ineptitude of generals and admirals. They denounce the crime as insensate folly of human strife.

Now, all this teaching ought to be very useful in preventing us from attacking or invading any other country, if anyone outside a madhouse wished to do so, but how would it help us if we were attacked or invaded ourselves? That is the question we have to ask.

Would the invaders consent to visit Lord Beaverbrook's exhibition, or listen to the impassioned appeals of Mr Lloyd George? Would they agree to meet that famous South African, General Smuts, and have their inferiority complex removed in friendly, reasonable debate? I doubt it. I have borne responsibility for the safety of this country in grievous times. I gravely doubt it.

But even if they did, I am not so sure we should convince them, and persuade them to go back quietly home. They might say, it seems to me: 'you are rich; we are poor. You seem well fed; we are hungry. You have been victorious; we have been defeated. You have valuable colonies; we have none. You have your navy; where is ours? You have had the past; let us have the future.' Above all, I fear they would say: 'you are weak and we are strong.'

There are those who say: 'Let us ignore the continent of Europe. Let us leave it with its hatreds and its armaments, to stew in its own juice, to fight out its own quarrels and decree its own doom. Let us turn our backs on this melancholy and alarming theme. Let us fix our gaze across the ocean and lead our own life in the midst of our peace-loving dominions and empires.'

Now, there would be much to be said for this plan if only we could unfasten the British islands from their rock foundations, and could tow them three thousand miles across the Atlantic Ocean and could anchor them safely upon the smiling coasts of Canada; but I have not yet heard of any way in which this could be done. No engineer has come forward with any scheme; even our best scientists are dumb. It would certainly, in any case, take a long time; have we got a long time?

A Hush Over Europe

In 1939, Churchill was trying to impress on the United States the true meaning to that country of the events that were to unfold soon in Europe. A transatlantic radio broadcast on 8 August contained these words:

There is a hush over all Europe, nay, over all the world, broken only by the dull thud of Japanese bombs falling on Chinese cities, on Chinese universities or near British and American ships ...
What kind of a hush is it? Alas! it is the hush of suspense, and in many lands it is the hush of fear. Listen! No, listen carefully; I think I hear something – yes, there it was quite clear. Don't you hear it? It is the tramp of armies crunching the gravel of the parade grounds, splashing through rain-soaked fields, the tramp of two million German soldiers and more than a million Italians – 'going on manoeuvres' – yes, only

on manoeuvres! Of course it's only manoeuvres, just like last year. After all, the dictators must train their soldiers.

They could scarcely do less in common prudence, when the Danes, the Dutch, the Swiss, the Albanians and of course the Jews may leap out upon them at any moment and rob them of their living space, and make them sign another paper to say who began it. Besides, these German and Italian armies may have another work of liberation to perform.

It was only last year they liberated Austria from the horrors of self-government. It was only in March they freed the Czechoslovak republic from the misery of independent existence. It is only two years ago that Signor Mussolini gave the ancient kingdom of Abyssinia its Magna Carta. It is only two months ago that little Albania got its writ of habeas corpus, and Mussolini sent in his bill of rights for King Zog to pay ...

No wonder the armies are tramping on when there is so much liberation to be done, and no wonder there is a hush among all the neighbours of Germany and Italy while they are wondering which one is going to be 'liberated' next.

The Storms of War

On 3 September 1939, Britain and France declared war on Germany. That same day, Churchill addressed the House of Commons:

In this solemn hour it is a consolation to recall and to dwell upon our repeated efforts for peace. All have been ill-starred, but all have been faithful and sincere. This is of the highest moral value — and not only moral value, but practical value — at the present time, because the wholehearted concurrence of scores of millions of men and women, whose co-operation is indispensable and whose comradeship and brotherhood are indispensable, is the only foundation upon which the trial and tribulation of modern war can be endured and surmounted.

This moral conviction alone affords that ever-fresh resilience which renews the strength and energy of people in long, doubtful and dark days. Outside, the storms of war may blow and the lands may be lashed with the fury of its gales, but in our own hearts this Sunday morning there is peace. Our hands may be active, but our consciences are at rest ...

This is not a question of fighting for Danzig or fighting for Poland. We are fighting to save the whole world from the pestilence of Nazi tyranny and in defence of all that is most sacred to man. This is no war of domination or imperial aggrandisement or material gain; no war to shut any country out of its sunlight and means of progress.

It is a war, viewed in its inherent quality, to establish, on impregnable rocks, the rights of the individual, and it is a war to establish and revive the stature of man.

Blood, Toil, Tears and Sweat

*On 13 May 1940, Churchill, three days into his
first tenure as prime minister, asked the House of
Commons for a vote of confidence in the all-party
administration he was putting together. His urgings
contained the following unforgettable words:*

On Friday evening last I received His Majesty's
commission to form a new administration. It was the
evident wish and will of parliament and the nation that
this should be conceived on the broadest possible basis
and that it should include all parties, both those who
supported the late government and also the parties of
the opposition.

I have completed the most important part of this
task. A war cabinet has been formed of five members,
representing, with the Liberal opposition, the unity
of the nation. The three party leaders have agreed to
serve, either in the war cabinet or in high executive
office. The three fighting services have been filled. It
was necessary that this should be done in one single
day, on account of the extreme urgency and rigour of
events.

To form an administration of this scale and
complexity is a serious undertaking in itself, but it must
be remembered that we are in the preliminary stage of
one of the greatest battles in history, that we are in
action at many points in Norway and in Holland, that
we have to be prepared in the Mediterranean, that the

air battle is continuous and that many preparations have to be made here at home.

In this crisis I hope I may be pardoned if I do not address the house at any length today. I hope that any of my friends and colleagues, or former colleagues, who are affected by the political reconstruction, will make all allowances for any lack of ceremony with which it has been necessary to act. I would say to the house, as I said to those who have joined this government: 'I have nothing to offer but blood, toil, tears and sweat.'

We have before us an ordeal of the most grievous kind. We have before us many, many long months of struggle and of suffering.

You ask, what is our policy? I will say: it is to wage war by sea, land and air, with all our might and with all the strength that God can give us; to wage war against a monstrous tyranny, never surpassed in the dark and lamentable catalogue of human crime. That is our policy.

You ask, what is our aim? I can answer in one word: victory; victory at all costs, victory in spite of all terror, victory however long and hard the road may be; for without victory, there is no survival. Let that be realised; no survival for the British Empire, no survival for all that the British Empire has stood for, no survival for the urge and impulse of the ages, that mankind will move forward towards its goal.

But I take up my task with buoyancy and hope. I feel sure that our cause will not be suffered to fail among men. At this time I feel entitled to claim the aid of all, and I say: 'Come then, let us go forward together with our united strength.'

In a Solemn Hour

Churchill made his first broadcast as prime minister on 19 May 1940, urging the British people: be ye men of valour.

I speak to you for the first time as prime minister in a solemn hour for the life of our country, of our empire, of our allies and, above all, of the cause of freedom.

A tremendous battle is raging in France and Flanders. The Germans, by a remarkable combination of air bombing and heavily armoured tanks, have broken through the French defences north of the Maginot Line, and strong columns of their armoured vehicles are ravaging the open country, which for the first day or two was without defenders. They have penetrated deeply and spread alarm and confusion in their track.

Behind them there are now appearing infantry in lorries, and behind them, again, the large masses are moving forward. The regroupment of the French armies to make head against, and also to strike at, this intruding wedge has been proceeding for several days, largely assisted by the magnificent efforts of the Royal Air Force.

We must not allow ourselves to be intimidated by the presence of these armoured vehicles in unexpected places behind our lines. If they are behind our front, the French are also at many points fighting actively behind theirs. Both sides are therefore in an extremely dangerous position.

And if the French army, and our own army, are well handled, as I believe they will be; if the French retain that genius for recovery and counter-attack for which they have so long been famous; and if the British army shows the dogged endurance and solid fighting power of which there have been so many examples in the past – then a sudden transformation of the scene might spring into being.

It would be foolish, however, to disguise the gravity of the hour. It would be still more foolish to lose heart and courage or to suppose that well-trained, well-equipped armies numbering three or four millions of men can be overcome in the space of a few weeks, or even months, by a scoop, or raid of mechanised vehicles, however formidable.

We may look with confidence to the stabilisation of the front in France, and to the general engagement of the masses, which will enable the qualities of the French and British soldiers to be matched squarely against those of their adversaries.

For myself, I have invincible confidence in the French army and its leaders. Only a very small part of that splendid army has yet been heavily engaged; and only a very small part of France has yet been invaded. There is a good evidence to show that practically the whole of the specialised and mechanised forces of the enemy have been already thrown into the battle; and we know that very heavy losses have been inflicted upon them.

No officer or man, no brigade or division which grapples at close quarters with the enemy, wherever encountered, can fail to make a worthy contribution to the general result. The armies must cast away the idea of resisting attack behind concrete lines or natural obstacles, and must realise that mastery can only be regained by furious and unrelenting assault. And this spirit must not only animate the high command, but must inspire every fighting man.

In the air – often at serious odds, often at odds hitherto thought overwhelming – we have been clawing down three or four to one of our enemies; and the relative balance of the British and German air forces is now considerably more favourable to us than at the beginning of the battle.

In cutting down the German bombers, we are fighting our own battle as well as that of France. My confidence in our ability to fight it out to the finish with the German air force has been strengthened by the fierce encounters which have taken place and are taking place. At the same time, our heavy bombers are striking nightly at the taproot of German mechanised power, and have already inflicted serious damage upon the oil refineries on which the Nazi effort to dominate the world directly depends.

We must expect that as soon as stability is reached on the western front, the bulk of that hideous apparatus of aggression which gashed Holland into ruin and slavery in a few days will be turned upon us. I am sure I speak for all when I say we are ready to face it; to endure it; and to retaliate against it, to any extent that the unwritten laws of war permit.

There will be many men and many women in this island who when the ordeal comes upon them, as come it will, will feel comfort, and even a pride, that they are sharing the perils of our lads at the front – soldiers, sailors and airmen, God bless them – and are drawing away from them a part at least of the onslaught they have to bear.

Is not this the appointed time for all to make the utmost exertions in their power? If the battle is to be won, we must provide our men with ever-increasing quantities of the weapons and ammunition they need. We must have, and have quickly, more aeroplanes, more tanks, more shells, more guns. There is imperious need for these vital munitions. They increase our strength against the powerfully armed enemy. They replace the wastage of the obstinate struggle; and the knowledge that wastage will speedily be replaced enables us to draw more readily upon our reserves and throw them in now that everything counts so much.

Our task is not only to win the battle, but to win the war. After this battle in France abates its force, there will come the battle for our island – for all that Britain is, and all that Britain means. That will be the struggle.

In that supreme emergency we shall not hesitate to take every step, even the most drastic, to call forth from our people the last ounce and the last inch of effort of which they are capable. The interests of property, the hours of labour, are nothing compared with the struggle for life and honour, for right and freedom, to which we have vowed ourselves.

I have received from the chiefs of the French Republic, and in particular from its indomitable prime minister, Monsieur Reynaud, the most sacred pledges that whatever happens they will fight to the end, be it bitter or be it glorious. Nay, if we fight to the end, it can only be glorious.

Having received His Majesty's commission, I have formed an administration of men and women of every party and of almost every point of view. We have differed and quarrelled in the past; but now one bond unites us all – to wage war until victory is won, and never to surrender ourselves to servitude and shame, whatever the cost and the agony may be.

This is one of the most awe-striking periods in the long history of France and Britain. It is also beyond doubt the most sublime. Side by side, unaided except by their kith and kin in the great dominions and by the wide empires which rest beneath their shield – side by side, the British and French peoples have advanced to rescue not only Europe but mankind from the foulest and most soul-destroying tyranny which has ever darkened and stained the pages of history.

Behind them, behind us, behind the armies and fleets of Britain and France, gather a group of shattered states and bludgeoned races – the Czechs, the Poles,

the Norwegians, the Danes, the Dutch, the Belgians –
upon all of whom the long night of barbarism will
descend, unbroken even by a star of hope, unless we
conquer, as conquer we must; as conquer we shall.

Today is Trinity Sunday. Centuries ago, words were
written to be a call and a spur to the faithful servants
of truth and justice: 'Arm yourselves, and be ye men of
valour, and be in readiness for the conflict; for it is better
for us to perish in battle than to look upon the outrage of
our nation and our altar. As the will of God is in heaven,
even so let it be.'

A Colossal Military Disaster ... We Shall Fight on the Beaches

Churchill told the Commons on 4 June 1940 that
recent events in France and Denmark, culminating
in the evacuation of more than 330,000 Allied troops
from Dunkirk, had been a massive disaster. Britain
now faced the possibility of invasion.

When, a week ago today, I asked the house to fix this
afternoon as the occasion for a statement, I feared it
would be my hard lot to announce the greatest military
disaster in our long history. I thought – and some good
judges agreed with me – that perhaps twenty or thirty
thousand men might be re-embarked. But it certainly
seemed that the whole of the French First Army and
the whole of the British Expeditionary Force north of
the Amiens-Abbeville gap would be broken up in the

open field or else would have to capitulate for lack of food and ammunition.

These were the hard and heavy tidings for which I called upon the house and the nation to prepare themselves a week ago. The whole root and core and brain of the British army, on which and around which we were to build, and are to build, the great British armies in the later years of the war, seemed about to perish upon the field or be led into an ignominious and starving captivity.

The enemy attacked us on all sides with great strength and fierceness, and their main power, the power of their far more numerous air force, was thrown into the battle or else concentrated upon Dunkirk and the beaches.

Pressing in upon the narrow exit, both from the east and from the west, the enemy began to fire with cannon upon the beaches by which alone the shipping could approach or depart. They sowed magnetic mines in the channels and seas; they sent repeated waves of hostile aircraft, sometimes more than a hundred strong in one formation, to cast their bombs upon the single pier that remained, and upon the sand dunes on which the troops had their only shelter. Their U-boats, one of which was sunk, and their motor launches took their toll of the vast traffic which now began.

For four or five days an intense struggle reigned. All their armoured divisions – or what was left of them – together with great masses of infantry and artillery, hurled themselves in vain upon the ever-narrowing, ever-contracting appendix within which the British and French armies fought.

Meanwhile, the Royal Navy, with the willing help of countless merchant seamen, strained every nerve to embark the British and Allied troops; two hundred and twenty light warships and six hundred and fifty other vessels were engaged. They had to operate upon the difficult coast, often in adverse weather, under an almost ceaseless hail of bombs and an increasing concentration of artillery fire. Nor were the seas, as I have said, themselves free from mines and torpedoes.

It was in conditions such as these that our men carried on, with little or no rest, for days and nights on end, making trip after trip across the dangerous waters, bringing with them always men whom they had rescued. The numbers they have brought back are the measure of their devotion and their courage. The hospital ships, which brought off many thousands of British and French wounded, being so plainly marked, were a special target for Nazi bombs; but the men and women on board them never faltered in their duty.

Meanwhile, the Royal Air Force, which had already been intervening in the battle, so far as its range would allow, from our home bases, now used part of its main metropolitan fighter strength, and struck at the German bombers and at the fighters which in large numbers protected them. This struggle was protracted and fierce.

Suddenly the scene has cleared, the crash and thunder has for the moment – but only for the moment – died away. A miracle of deliverance, achieved by valour, by perseverance, by perfect discipline, by faultless service, by resource, by skill, by unconquerable fidelity, is manifest to us all. The enemy was hurled back by the retreating British troops. He was so roughly handled that he did not harry their departure seriously.

Sir, we must be very careful not to assign to this deliverance the attributes of a victory. Wars are not won by evacuations. But there was a victory inside this deliverance, which should be noted. It was gained by the air force. Many of our soldiers coming back have not seen the air force at work; they saw only the bombers which escaped its protective attack. They under-rate its achievements. I have heard much talk of this; that is why I go out of my way to say this. I will tell you about it.

This was a great trial of strength between the British and German air forces. Can you conceive a greater objective for the Germans in the air than to make evacuation from these beaches impossible, and to sink all these ships which were displayed, almost to the extent of thousands? Could there have been an objective of greater military importance and significance for the whole purpose of the war than this? They tried hard, and they were beaten back; they were frustrated in their task. We got the army away; and they have paid fourfold for any losses which they have inflicted.

When we consider how much greater would be our advantage in defending the air above this island against an overseas attack, I must say that I find in these facts a sure basis upon which practical and reassuring thoughts may rest. I will pay my tribute to these young airmen.

The great French army was very largely, for the time being, cast back and disturbed by the onrush of a few thousands of armoured vehicles. May it not also be that the cause of civilisation itself will be defended by the skill and devotion of a few thousand airmen?

There never has been, I suppose, in all the world, in all the history of war, such an opportunity for youth. The knights of the round table, the crusaders, all fall back into the past – not only distant but prosaic; these young men, going forth every morn to guard their native land and all that we stand for, holding in their hands these instruments of colossal and shattering power, of whom it may be said that:

Every morn brought forth a noble chance, and every chance brought forth a noble knight, deserve our gratitude, as do all the brave men who, in so many ways and on so many occasions, are ready, and continue ready to give life and all for their native land.

Nevertheless, our thankfulness at the escape of our army and so many men, whose loved ones have passed through an agonising week, must not blind us to the fact that what happened in France and Belgium is a colossal military disaster.

The French army has been weakened, the Belgian army has been lost, a large part of those fortified lines upon which so much faith had been reposed is gone, many valuable mining districts and factories have passed into the enemy's possession, the whole of the Channel ports are in his hands, with all the tragic consequences that follow from that, and we must expect another blow to be struck almost immediately at us or at France.

We are told that Herr Hitler has a plan for invading the British Isles. This has often been thought of before. When Napoleon lay at Boulogne for a year with his flat-bottomed boats and his Grand Army, he was told by someone: 'There are bitter weeds in England'. There are certainly a great many more of them since the British Expeditionary Force returned.

I have, myself, full confidence that if all do their duty, if nothing is neglected, and if the best arrangements are made, as they are being made, we shall prove ourselves once more able to defend our island home, to ride out the storm of war, and to outlive the menace of tyranny, if necessary for years, if necessary alone.

At any rate, that is what we are going to try to do. That is the resolve of His Majesty's government – every man of them. That is the will of parliament and the nation. The British Empire and the French Republic, linked together in their cause and in their need, will defend to the death their native soil, aiding each other like good comrades to the utmost of their strength.

We shall go on to the end, we shall fight in France, we shall fight on the seas and oceans, we shall fight with growing confidence and growing strength in the air, we shall defend our island, whatever the cost may be. We shall fight on the beaches, we shall fight on the landing grounds, we shall fight in the fields and in the streets, we shall fight in the hills; we shall never surrender, and if, which I do not for a moment believe, this island or a large part of it were subjugated and starving, then our empire beyond the seas, armed and guarded by the British fleet, would carry on the struggle, until, in God's good time, the new world, with all its power and might, steps forth to the rescue and the liberation of the old.

This was Their Finest Hour

Two weeks after his 'fight on the beaches' speech, on 18 June 1940, Churchill again addressed the Commons.

I am happy to inform the house that our fighter strength is stronger at the present time relatively to the Germans, who have suffered terrible losses, than it has ever been; and consequently we believe ourselves possessed of the capacity to continue the war in the air under better conditions than we have ever experienced before. I look forward confidently to the exploits of our fighter pilots – these splendid men, this brilliant youth – who will have the glory of saving their native land, their island home, and all they love, from the most deadly of all attacks.

There remains, of course, the danger of bombing attacks, which will certainly be made very soon upon us by the bomber forces of the enemy. It is true that the German bomber force is superior in numbers to ours; but we have a very large bomber force also, which we shall use to strike at military targets in Germany without intermission.

I do not at all under-rate the severity of the ordeal which lies before us; but I believe our countrymen will show themselves capable of standing up to it, like the brave men of Barcelona, and will be able to stand up to it, and carry on in spite of it, at least as well as any other people in the world. Much will depend upon this; every man and every woman will have the chance to show the finest qualities of their race, and render the highest service to their cause.

I have thought it right upon this occasion to give the house and the country some indication of the solid, practical grounds upon which we base our inflexible resolve to continue the war. There are a good many people who say: 'Never mind. Win or lose, sink or swim, better die than submit to tyranny – and such a tyranny.' And I do not dissociate myself from them.

But I can assure them that our professional advisers of the three services unitedly advise that we should carry on the war, and that there are good and reasonable hopes of final victory.

We have fully informed and consulted all the self-governing dominions, these great communities far beyond the oceans who have been built up on our laws and on our civilisation, and who are absolutely free to choose their course, but are absolutely devoted to the ancient motherland, and who feel themselves inspired by the same emotions which lead me to stake our all upon duty and honour.

During the first four years of the last war, the Allies experienced nothing but disaster and disappointment. That was our constant fate: one blow after another, terrible losses, frightful dangers. Everything miscarried. And yet at the end of those four years the morale of the Allies was higher than that of the Germans, who had moved from one aggressive triumph to another, and who stood everywhere triumphant invaders of the lands into which they had broken.

During that war we repeatedly asked ourselves the question: how are we going to win? And no one was able ever to answer it with much precision, until at the end, quite suddenly, quite unexpectedly, our terrible foe collapsed before us, and we were so glutted with victory that in our folly we threw it away.

We do not yet know what will happen in France or whether the French resistance will be prolonged, both in France and in the French empire overseas. The French government will be throwing away great opportunities and casting adrift their future if they do not continue the war in accordance with their treaty obligations, from which we have not felt able to release them.

The house will have read the historic declaration in which, at the desire of many Frenchmen – and of our own hearts – we have proclaimed our willingness at the darkest hour in French history to conclude a union of common citizenship in this struggle. However matters may go in France or with the French government, or other French governments, we in this island and in the British Empire will never lose our sense of comradeship with the French people.

If we are now called upon to endure what they have been suffering, we shall emulate their courage, and if final victory rewards our toils they shall share the gains, aye, and freedom shall be restored to all. We abate nothing of our just demands; not one jot or tittle do we recede. Czechs, Poles, Norwegians, Dutch, Belgians have joined their causes to our own. All these shall be restored.

What General Weygand called the Battle of France is over. I expect that the Battle of Britain is about to begin. Upon this battle depends the survival of Christian civilisation. Upon it depends our own British life, and the long continuity of our institutions and our empire. The whole fury and might of the enemy must very soon be turned on us.

Hitler knows that he will have to break us in this island or lose the war. If we can stand up to him, all Europe may be free and the life of the world may move forward into broad, sunlit uplands. But if we fail, then the whole world, including the United States, including all that we have known and cared for, will sink into the abyss of a new dark age made more sinister, and perhaps more protracted, by the lights of perverted science.

Let us therefore brace ourselves to our duties, and so bear ourselves that, if the British Empire and its commonwealth last for a thousand years, men will still say: 'This was their finest hour.'

The Unknown Warriors

In the summer of 1940, as the Luftwaffe began its struggle to achieve air supremacy in anticipation of the invasion of Britain, it was met by stern resistance from the Royal Air Force. The Battle of Britain had begun. Churchill broadcast to the nation on July 14.

This is no war of chieftains or of princes, of dynasties or national ambition; it is a war of peoples and of causes. There are vast numbers, not only in this island but in every land, who will render faithful service in this war, but whose names will never be known, whose deeds will never be recorded.

This is a war of the unknown warriors; but let all strive without failing in faith or in duty, and the dark curse of Hitler will be lifted from our age.

The First Year ... the Few

In a speech to the House of Commons on 20 August 1940, as the Battle of Britain was reaching its critical stage, Churchill paid tribute to the RAF and its brilliant fighter pilots.

The great air battle which has been in progress over this island for the last few weeks has recently attained a high intensity. It is too soon to attempt to assign limits either to its scale or to its duration. We must certainly expect that greater efforts will be made by the enemy than any he has put forth. Hostile airfields are still being developed in France and the Low Countries, and the movement of squadrons and material for attacking us is still proceeding.

It is quite plain that Herr Hitler could not admit defeat in his air attack on Great Britain without sustaining most serious injury. If, after all his boastings and blood-curdling threats and lurid accounts trumpeted round the world of the damage he has inflicted, of the vast numbers of our air force he has shot down, so he says, with so little loss to himself; if after tales of the panic-stricken British crushed in their holes cursing the plutocratic parliament which has led them to such a plight; if after all this his whole air onslaught were forced after a while tamely to peter out, the Führer's reputation for veracity of statement might be seriously impugned.

We may be sure, therefore, that he will continue as long as he has the strength to do so, and as long as any preoccupations he may have in respect of the Russian air force allow him to do so.

On the other hand, the conditions and course of the fighting have so far been favourable to us. I told the house two months ago that whereas in France our fighter aircraft were wont to inflict a loss of two or three to one upon the Germans, and in the fighting at Dunkirk, which was a kind of no man's land, a loss of about three or four to one, we expected that in an attack on this island we should achieve a larger ratio. This has certainly come true.

It must also be remembered that all the enemy machines and pilots which are shot down over our island, or over the seas which surround it, are either destroyed or captured; whereas a considerable proportion of our machines, and also of our pilots, are saved, and soon again in many cases come into action.

The gratitude of every home in our island, in our empire, and indeed throughout the world, except in the abodes of the guilty, goes out to the British airmen who, undaunted by odds, unwearied in their constant challenge and mortal danger, are turning the tide of the world war by their prowess and by their devotion. Never in the field of human conflict was so much owed by so many to so few.

All our hearts go out to the fighter pilots, whose brilliant actions we see with our own eyes day after day; but we must never forget that all the time, night after night, month after month, our bomber squadrons travel far into Germany, find their targets in the darkness by the highest navigational skill, aim their attacks, often under the heaviest fire, often with serious loss, with deliberate, careful discrimination, and inflict shattering blows upon the whole of the technical and war-making structure of the Nazi power.

On no part of the Royal Air Force does the weight of the war fall more heavily than on the daylight bombers who will play an invaluable part in the case of invasion and whose unflinching zeal it has been necessary in the meanwhile on numerous occasions to restrain.

I hope – indeed I pray – that we shall not be found unworthy of our victory if, after toil and tribulation, it is granted to us. For the rest, we have to gain the victory. That is our task.

There is, however, one direction in which we can see a little more clearly ahead. We have to think not only for ourselves but for the lasting security of the cause and principles for which we are fighting, and of the long future of the British commonwealth of nations.

Some months ago, we came to the conclusion that the interests of the United States and of the British Empire both required that the United States should have facilities for the naval and air defence of the western hemisphere against the attack of a Nazi power which might have acquired temporary but lengthy control of a large part of western Europe and its formidable resources.

We had therefore decided spontaneously, and without being asked or offered any inducement, to inform the government of the United States that we would be glad to place such defence facilities at their disposal by leasing suitable sites in our transatlantic possessions for their greater security against the unmeasured dangers of the future.

The principle of association of interests for common purposes between Great Britain and the United States had developed even before the war. Various agreements had been reached about certain small islands in the

Pacific Ocean which had become important as air fuelling points. In all this line of thought we found ourselves in very close harmony with the government of Canada.

Presently we learned that anxiety was also felt in the United States about the air and naval defence of their Atlantic seaboard, and president Roosevelt has recently made it clear that he would like to discuss with us, and with the dominion of Canada and with Newfoundland, the development of American naval and air facilities in Newfoundland and in the West Indies.

There is, of course, no question of any transference of sovereignty – that has never been suggested – or of any action being taken without the consent, or against the wishes of, the various colonies concerned, but for our part, His Majesty's government are entirely willing to accord defence facilities to the United States on a 99 years leasehold basis, and we feel sure that our interests no less than theirs, and the interests of the colonies themselves and of Canada and Newfoundland will be served thereby.

These are important steps. Undoubtedly this process means that these two great organisations of the English-speaking democracies, the British Empire and the United States, will have to be somewhat mixed up together in some of their affairs for mutual and general advantage.

For my own part, looking out upon the future, I do not view the process with any misgivings. I could not stop it if I wished; no one can stop it. Like the Mississippi, it just keeps rolling along. Let it roll. Let it roll on full flood, inexorable, irresistible, benignant, to broader lands and better days.

Every Man to his Post

In early September 1940, the Luftwaffe started its bombing attacks on the populations of London and other major cities. On September 11, Churchill reasserted the determination of the British to prevail.

When I said in the House of Commons the other day that I thought it improbable that the enemy's air attack in September could be more than three times as great as it was in August, I was not, of course, referring to barbarous attacks upon the civil population, but to the great air battle which is being fought out between our fighters and the German air force.

This effort of the Germans to secure daylight mastery of the air over England is, of course, the crux of the whole war. So far it has failed conspicuously. It has cost them very dear, and we have felt stronger, and are actually and relatively, a good deal stronger, than when the hard fighting began in July.

There is no doubt that Herr Hitler is using up his fighter force at a very high rate, and that if he goes on for many more weeks he will wear down and ruin this vital part of his air force. That will give us a very great advantage.

On the other hand, for him to try to invade this country without having secured mastery in the air would be a very hazardous undertaking.

If this invasion is going to be tried at all, it does not seem that it can be long delayed. The weather may break at any time. Besides this, it is difficult for the enemy to keep these gatherings of ships waiting about indefinitely, while they are bombed every night by our bombers, and very often shelled by our warships which are waiting for them outside.

Therefore, we must regard the next week or so as a very important week for us in our history. It ranks with the days when the Spanish Armada was approaching the Channel, and Drake was finishing his game of bowls; or when Nelson stood between us and Napoleon's Grand Army at Boulogne. We have read about all this in the history books; but what is happening now is on a far greater scale and of far more consequence to the life and future of the world and its civilisation than these brave old days of the past.

Every man and woman will therefore prepare himself to do his duty, whatever it may be, with special pride and care. Our fleets and flotillas are very powerful and numerous; our air force is at the highest strength it has ever reached, and it is conscious of its proved superiority, not indeed in numbers, but in men and machines. Our shores are well fortified and strongly manned, and behind them, ready to attack the invaders, we have a far larger and better equipped mobile army than we have ever had before.

This is a time for everyone to stand together and hold firm, as they are doing. I express my admiration for the exemplary manner in which all the air raid precautions services of London are being discharged, especially the fire brigade, whose work has been so heavy and also dangerous. All the world that is still free marvels at the composure and fortitude with which the citizens of London are facing and surmounting the great ordeal to which they are subjected, the end of which or the severity of which cannot yet be foreseen.

It is a message of good cheer to our fighting forces on the seas, in the air, and in our waiting armies in all their posts and stations, that we send them from this capital city. They know that they have behind them a people who will not flinch or weary of the struggle, hard and protracted though it will be; but that we shall rather draw from the heart of suffering itself the means of inspiration and survival, and of a victory won not only for ourselves but for all; a victory won not only for our own time, but for the long and better days that are to come.

Give us the Tools

In the early days of the war, Churchill was ever hopeful that the United States would add its military might, in addition to the supplies it willingly gave, to the British cause. In early 1941 he received a visit from president Roosevelt's envoy, Wendell Willkie. Some days later, on February 9, he made a broadcast on the BBC.

A Nazi invasion of Great Britain last autumn would have been a more or less improvised affair. Hitler took it for granted that when France gave in we should give in; but we did not give in. And he had to think again.

An invasion now will be supported by a much more carefully prepared tackle and equipment of landing craft and other apparatus, all of which will have been planned and manufactured during the winter months. We must all be prepared to meet gas attacks, parachute attacks and glider attacks with constancy, forethought and practised skill.

In order to win the war, Hitler must destroy Great Britain. With every month that passes, the many proud and once happy countries he is now holding down by brute force and vile intrigue are learning to hate the Prussian yoke and the Nazi name as nothing has ever been hated so fiercely and so widely among men before. And all the time, masters of the sea and air, the British Empire – nay, in a certain sense, the whole English-speaking world – will be on his track, bearing with them the swords of justice.

The other day, president Roosevelt gave his opponent in the late presidential election [Wendell Willkie] a letter of introduction to me, and in it he wrote out a verse, in his own handwriting, from Longfellow, which he said, 'applies to you people as it does to us.' Here is the verse:

Sail on, O Ship of State!
Sail on, O Union, strong and great!
Humanity with all its fears,

With all the hopes of future years,
Is hanging breathless on thy fate!

What is the answer that I shall give, in your name, to this great man, the thrice-chosen head of a nation of a hundred and thirty millions? Here is the answer which I will give to president Roosevelt: put your confidence in us. Give us your faith and your blessing, and, under Providence, all will be well.

We shall not fail or falter; we shall not weaken or tire. Neither the sudden shock of battle, nor the long-drawn trials of vigilance and exertion will wear us down. Give us the tools, and we will finish the job.

Some Chicken ... Some Neck

In a speech to the Canadian parliament in 1942,
Churchill, to roars of laughter, recalled discussions
with the French:

When I warned them [the French] that Britain would fight on alone whatever they did, their generals told their prime minister and his divided cabinet: 'In three weeks, England will have her neck wrung like a chicken.'

Some chicken; some neck.

The End of the War in Europe

On 8 May 1945, Churchill addressed the nation.

Yesterday morning at 2.41am at general Eisenhower's headquarters, general Jodl, the representative of the German high command, and grand admiral Dönitz, the designated head of the German state, signed the act of unconditional surrender of all German land, sea and air forces in Europe to the Allied Expeditionary Force, and simultaneously to the Soviet high command.

General Bedell Smith, chief of staff of the United States army, and general François Sevez signed the document on behalf of the supreme commander of the Allied Expeditionary Force, and general Susloparov signed on behalf of the Russian high command.

Today this agreement will be ratified and confirmed at Berlin, where air chief marshal Tedder, deputy supreme commander of the Allied Expeditionary Force, and general de Lattre de Tassigny will sign on behalf of general Eisenhower. General Zhukov will sign on behalf of the Soviet high command. The German representatives will be field marshal Keitel, chief of the high command, and the commanders-in-chief of the German army, navy and air forces.

Hostilities will end officially at one minute after midnight tonight (Tuesday May 8), but in the interests of saving lives the 'ceasefire' began yesterday to be sounded all along the front, and our dear Channel Islands are also to be freed today.

The Germans are still in places resisting the Russian troops, but should they continue to do so after midnight they will, of course, deprive themselves of the protection of the laws of war, and will be attacked from all quarters by the allied troops. It is not surprising that on such long fronts and in the existing disorder of the enemy the commands of the German high command should not in every case be obeyed immediately.

This does not, in our opinion, with the best military advice at our disposal, constitute any reason for withholding from the nation the facts communicated to us by general Eisenhower of the unconditional surrender already signed at Rheims, nor should it prevent us from celebrating today and tomorrow (Wednesday) as Victory in Europe days.

Today, perhaps, we shall think mostly of ourselves. Tomorrow we shall pay a particular tribute to our heroic Russian comrades, whose prowess in the field has been one of the grand contributions to the general victory.

The German war is therefore at an end. After years of intense preparation, Germany hurled herself on Poland at the beginning of September 1939; and, in pursuance of our guarantee to Poland and in common with the French Republic, Great Britain, the British Empire and commonwealth of nations, declared war upon this foul aggression. After gallant France had been struck down, we from this island and from our united empire, maintained the struggle single-handed for a whole year until we were joined by the military might of Soviet Russia, and later by the overwhelming power and resources of the United States of America.

Finally, almost the whole world was combined against the evildoers, who are now prostrate before us. Our gratitude to all our splendid allies goes forth from all our hearts in this island and throughout the British Empire.

We may allow ourselves a brief period of rejoicing; but let us not forget for a moment the toil and efforts that lie ahead. Japan, with all her treachery and greed, remains unsubdued. The injury she has inflicted upon Great Britain, the United States and other countries, and her detestable cruelties, call for justice and retribution. We must now devote all our strength and resources to the completion of our task, both at home and abroad.

Advance, Britannia! Long live the cause of freedom! God save the king!

The Iron Curtain

Churchill, speaking at Westminster College in Fulton, Missouri on 5 March 1946, warned that Europe was once more divided.

Last time I saw it all coming and I cried aloud to my own fellow countrymen and to the world, but no one paid any attention. Up till the year 1933 or even 1935, Germany might have been saved from the awful fate which has overtaken her and we might all have been spared the miseries Hitler let loose upon mankind.

There never was a war in history easier to prevent by timely action than the one which has just desolated such great areas of the globe. It could have been prevented in my belief without the firing of a single shot, and Germany might be powerful, prosperous and honoured today; but no one would listen and one by one we were all sucked into the awful whirlpool.

We surely must not let that happen again.

>From Stettin in the Baltic to Trieste in the Adriatic, an iron curtain has descended across the continent. Behind that line lie all the capitals of the ancient states of central and eastern Europe. Warsaw, Berlin, Prague, Vienna, Budapest, Belgrade, Bucharest and Sofia, all these famous cities and the populations around them lie in what I must call the Soviet sphere.

What is needed is a settlement, and the longer this is delayed, the more difficult it will be and the greater our dangers will become.

>From what I have seen of our Russian friends and allies during the war, I am convinced that there is nothing they admire so much as strength, and there is nothing for which they have less respect than for weakness, especially military weakness.

CHAPTER 8

On Making War

Churchill's position as Britain's most feted war leader of the modern era was born of tireless study of the arts of war as well as fierce determination and, of course, a gift for the apt phrase.

*

'Never, never, never believe any war will be smooth and easy, or that anyone who embarks on the strange voyage can measure the tides and hurricanes he will encounter,' warned Churchill.

*

'The statesman who yields to war fever must realise that once the signal is given, he is no longer the master of policy but the slave of unforeseeable and uncontrollable events.'

*

'There is only one thing worse than fighting with allies, and that is fighting without them.'

*

Retreating was not in Churchill's nature. *'One ought never to turn one's back on a threatened danger and try to run away from it,'* he said. *'If you do that, you will double the danger. But if you meet it promptly and without flinching, you will reduce the danger by half. Never run away from anything. Never!'*

*

'No one can guarantee success in war, but only deserve it.'

*

In 1941, Churchill sent a very formal note to the Japanese ambassador in London, informing him of Britain's declaration of war upon Japan. *'Some people do not like this ceremonial style,'* he commented. *'But when you have to kill a man it costs nothing to be polite.'*

*

On air raids: *'Learn to get used to it. Eels get used to skinning.'*

*

Churchill habitually made short work of those who said that Britain should prepare only for a defensive war. *'I cannot subscribe to the idea that it might be possible to dig ourselves in and make no preparations for anything other than passive defence,'* he insisted. *'It is the theory of the turtle, which is disproved at every Lord Mayor's Banquet.'* Note: turtle soup was finally dropped from the menu of the Lord Mayor's banquet in 1971.

*

'In war you don't have to be nice; you only have to be right.'

*

During his military career, Churchill came under fire in Cuba, India, Africa and France. *'There is nothing more exhilarating than to be shot at without result,'* he observed.

*

'History is written by the victors.'

*

'For good or for ill, air mastery is today the supreme expression of military power and fleets and armies, however vital and important, must accept a subordinate rank.'

*

'I like a man who grins when he fights.'

*

'If the Almighty were to rebuild the world and asked me for advice, I would have English Channels round every country. And the atmosphere would be such that anything which attempted to fly would be set on fire.'

*

Then there was a multitude of Churchillian one-liners on war:

*

'In war as in life, it is often necessary when some cherished scheme has failed, to take up the best alternative open, and if so, it is folly not to work for it with all your might.'

*

On Making War

'In wartime, truth is so precious that she should always be attended by a bodyguard of lies.'

*

'A prisoner of war is a man who tries to kill you and fails, and then asks you not to kill him.'

*

'Battles are won by slaughter and manoeuvre. The greater the general, the more he contributes in manoeuvre, the less he demands in slaughter.'

*

'The great defence against the air menace is to attack the enemy's aircraft as near as possible to their point of departure.'

*

'The problems of victory are more agreeable than those of defeat, but they are no less difficult.'

*

'Those who can win a war well can rarely make a good peace and those who could make a good peace would never have won the war.'

*

'To jaw-jaw is always better than to war-war.'

*

'War is a game that is played with a smile. If you can't smile, grin. If you can't grin, keep out of the way till you can.'

*

'War is mainly a catalogue of blunders.'

*

'When you are winning a war almost everything that happens can be claimed to be right and wise.'

CHAPTER 9

Prime Minister in Peace

After the Labour general election victory of 1945, Churchill became prime minister again in 1951. Churchill once described the office of prime minister as unique.

*

'If he trips he must be sustained; if he makes mistakes they must be covered; if he sleeps he must not be wantonly disturbed; if he is no good he must be poleaxed.'

*

A statue of general Charles Gordon – known as Chinese Gordon and best remembered for campaigns in China and north Africa – was kept in store during the war. Afterwards, minister of works David Eccles wanted it to be moved and put up in Hyde Park. Churchill rebuked him: *'Oh! Don't be in such a hurry, minister of works. Don't you know there are only two things which the British people care deeply about – cruelty to animals and the moving of public statues?'*

*

After being re-elected prime minister in 1951, Churchill was on his way to Venice by train, and, anxious to catch the first possible glimpse of the city as he approached, leant far out of the window. Suddenly his detective, who accompanied him everywhere, wrenched him back by the shoulder, and a split second later a concrete pylon bearing the overhead wires for the electric railway flashed by, about a foot from the side of the train. Coolly, Churchill smiled. *'Anthony Eden nearly got a new job then,'* he observed.

*

When Eccles became minister of works in 1951, he discovered plans left by the Labour government to excavate vast underground chambers to be used as government headquarters in the event of a third world war. Churchill killed the whole project by making it appear quite ridiculous.

Churchill: *'You say that this hole is "to accommodate the key services of the government in the next war". How many of us will work down there?'*

Eccles: *'The estimate was seventeen thousand.'*

Churchill: *'Seventeen thousand! And who, pray, will get our breakfast?'*

*

Churchill had just conducted his last cabinet meeting on the eve of his retirement as prime minister in 1955. The farewell speeches had been made. There was a long pause, nobody trusting himself to speak. Churchill slowly looked round at his colleagues. *'Sir Norman Brook, with his customary foresight, has arranged for a photographer to take our picture upstairs. Let us go. We are not a bad-looking lot.'*

*

Lord Eccles gave typical examples of Churchill's humour in greeting his colleagues at cabinet meetings:

*

'You seem very sad, chancellor of the exchequer. I don't know why. There is nothing about money before us today.'

*

'Good morning, my dear minister of agriculture. I see you've been talking in the country about hops. I do hope that doesn't mean we haven't got any.'

*

After his electoral victory of 1951, Churchill said at the Lord Mayor's banquet at the Guildhall: 'This is the first occasion when I have addressed this assembly here as a prime minister. The explanation is convincing. When I should have come here as prime minister, the Guildhall was blown up, and before it was repaired I was blown out.'

*

'This Treasury paper, by its very length, defends itself against the risk of being read.'

CHAPTER 10

The Political Life

Churchill relished the cut and thrust of the political arena, and his wit and wisdom were always ready to show themselves in even the least promising situations.

*

Very early in his career, Churchill told a gathering of journalists: *'For my own part I have always felt that a politician is to be judged by the animosities which he excites among his opponents. I have always set myself not merely to relish but to deserve thoroughly their censure.'*

*

'You have enemies? Good. That means you've stood up for something, some time in your life.'

*

In 1922, Churchill was campaigning for election in Dundee when he was stricken by appendicitis. He subsequently came bottom of the poll. *'In the twinkling of an eye I found myself without an office, without a seat, without a party and without an appendix,'* he commented later.

*

'Politics is not a game. It is an earnest business.'

*

When the Conservatives were defeated at the 1945 general election, Churchill remarked ruefully: *'My wife said: "It may well be a blessing in disguise". I replied: "At the moment it seems quite effectively disguised."'*

*

Churchill condemned the government of Neville Chamberlain (from 1937 to 1940) thus: *'They are decided only to be undecided, resolved to be irresolute, adamant for drift, all-powerful for impotence.'*

*

'I'm just preparing my impromptu remarks.'

*

On a tour of America, Churchill was stopped by a woman who said in a gushing voice: **'Doesn't it thrill you, Mr Churchill, to know that every time you make a speech the hall is packed to overflowing?'** *'It is quite flattering,'* Winston replied. *'But whenever I feel this way I always remember that, if instead of making a political speech, I was being hanged, the crowd would be twice as big.'*

*

Churchill always insisted that he did what he did for the good of the people. When he was asked in 1908 if he did not enjoy immensely the whole atmosphere of politics – the speeches, the crowds, the sense of increasing power – he answered: *'Of course I do. Thou shalt not muzzle the ox when he treadeth out the corn. That shall be my plea on the day of judgement.'*

*

'The inherent vice of capitalism is the unequal sharing of blessings; the inherent virtue of socialism is the equal sharing of miseries.'

*

Churchill, as home secretary, made a point of being at the scene of the so-called Battle of Sidney Street, a 1911 incident when Latvian revolutionaries shot at police in a murderous siege. Newsreel cameras captured the moment when a bullet ripped through Churchill's top hat. His involvement caused immense controversy, and at one stage his under-secretary, Charles Masterman, burst angrily into his room. **'What the hell have you been doing, Winston?'** he demanded. The reply came in Churchill's characteristic lisp: *'Now, Charlie. Don't be cross, it was such fun.'*

*

When Churchill was in the political wilderness during the 1930s, a friend asked him: **'Don't you think No 10 Downing Street would be a lovely place to live?'** The former chancellor of the exchequer replied: *'No I don't. I have lived next door to it long enough.'*

*

It was between 1924 and 1929 that Churchill served as chancellor of the exchequer. His appointment had been regarded as surprising and at the end of his term of office he himself remarked: *'Everybody said I was the worst chancellor of the exchequer that ever was.'* There was a long pause, followed by: *'And I am now inclined to agree with them.'*

*

In 1924, Churchill left the Liberal party to return to the Conservatives. *'Anyone can rat,'* he remarked, *'but it takes a certain amount of ingenuity to re-rat.'*

*

>From his earliest days in politics, Churchill's beliefs were forthright. He declared: *'England would gain far more from the rising tide of Tory democracy than from the dried-up drainpipe of radicalism.'*

*

'I always avoid prophesying beforehand, because it is a much better policy to prophesy after the event has already taken place.'

CHAPTER 11

Family Life

Churchill and Clementine Hozier were married in
1908 and they had five children. From 1922 until
his death in 1965, the Churchill family home was
Chartwell, near Westerham in Kent.

*

*'Where does the family start? It starts with a young
man falling in love with a girl. No superior alternative
has yet been found.'*

*

Churchill's valet, Norman McGowan, was surprised
when he first joined the household to hear Churchill
muttering in his bath. McGowan thought that he was
talking to him and called out: **'Do you want me?'**

'I wasn't talking to you, Norman,' Churchill replied. *'I
was addressing the House of Commons.'*

*

Churchill would often sit alone for hours on end in the cabinet room of 10 Downing Street, and his valet would bring him in some soup. His poodle Rufus, having realised what the valet was up to, would follow him into the cabinet room. Winston would then stoop down to pet the dog, saying: *'You know, Rufus, you're not a member of the cabinet, nor of the civil service, so by what right do you come into the cabinet room?'*

*

Churchill's first child, Diana, was born in 1909. David Lloyd George asked him: **'Is she a pretty child?'** Winston smiled: *'The prettiest child ever seen.'* **'Like her mother, I suppose,'** suggested Lloyd George. *'No,'* retorted Winston. *'She is the image of me.'*

*

Churchill had a passion for fresh cream. He would often empty a whole jug by himself and then look round the table and ask pugnaciously: *'Does anyone want cream?'*

*

When Clementine arrived back at Chartwell from London, it was often her custom to enter the front hall shouting: **'Wow! Wow!'** After a few seconds an answering bellow – *'Wow! Wow!'* – would come back from Winston.

*

'My wife and I tried two or three times in the last forty years to have breakfast together, but it was so disagreeable we had to stop.'

CHAPTER 12

Days in the Life

Despite suffering from depression, which he named the Black Dog, for long periods of his life, a smile was seldom far from Churchill's lips.

*

One of Churchill's wartime personal assistants once delivered to him a mysterious box from the intelligence agency MI5, and was surprised to hear loud chuckles coming from the prime minister's room. He went in and found Churchill sporting a bright red beard and luxuriant side-whiskers. *'A very effective disguise, you will agree,'* said Winston. *'I think I shall go and see the king in it this afternoon.'*

*

During a visit to Palm Beach, Florida in 1941, Churchill was about to go for a swim when his detective (nowadays called a bodyguard) told him that a shark had been seen in the vicinity. It was not a dangerous kind, the detective added. *'I am not so sure about that,'* said Churchill over his shoulder, as he dived in. *'I must see his identity card before I trust myself to him.'*

*

Once, when Churchill was staying at the White House with president Roosevelt, the president made his way after breakfast to Churchill's room, expecting the prime minister to be ready for an important appointment. Roosevelt knocked politely on Churchill's door and entered the bedroom, only to retreat hastily: the prime minister was standing there naked, having just got out of his bath. *'Do come in, mister president,'* Churchill called, with not a hint of embarrassment. *'The prime minister of Great Britain has nothing to hide from the president of the United States.'*

*

In 1942, Churchill addressed Allied troops in the Roman amphitheatre at Carthage, Tunisia: *'I am speaking from where the cries of Christian virgins rent the air whilst roaring lions devoured them. And yet I am no lion – and certainly not a virgin.'*

*

He told the United States Congress during a visit to Washington in 1942: *'I cannot help reflecting that if my father had been American and my mother British, instead of the other way round, I might have got here on my own.'*

*

In 1951, Churchill was asked to address the Royal College of Physicians on the occasion of the presentation of a portrait of Lord Moran, his personal doctor, by the celebrated Italian painter Pietro Annigoni. Churchill was by then already an Honorary Surgeon and had now been made an Honorary Fellow of the Royal College of Physicians. But *'unless there is a very marked shortage of capable men in both these professions,'* he told his audience, *'I shall not press myself upon you.'*

*

A photographer, who had come to take a birthday photograph of Churchill, said to him: **'I hope, sir, that I will shoot your picture on your hundredth birthday.'** Winston surveyed the man briefly. *'I don't see why not, young man,'* he replied. *'You look reasonably fit and healthy.'*

*

During World War II, the archbishop of Canterbury was not completely satisfied that every precaution had been taken to safeguard his cathedral and its priceless treasures. Churchill assured him that everything possible had been done, but the archbishop insisted: **'What will happen if they score a direct hit on the cathedral?'** Churchill was by this time irritated, and his reply was rather short: *'In that case, my dear archbishop, you will have to regard it as a divine summons.'*

*

In the late 1920s and 1930s, Churchill spent time in the political wilderness, removed from public office. Once, when Stanley Baldwin was prime minister, the sombre Churchill surveyed Chartwell Manor, his house, and said: *'I suppose these bricks will be excavated in five hundred years' time as a relic of Stanley Badwin's England.'*

*

Once, Churchill was meeting the officers of the Cinque Ports, a grouping of coastal towns in Kent and Sussex of which he was the ceremonial warden. One of the epaulettes on his uniform fell off, and he was forced to continue his tour of duty minus one epaulette. Later he grinned: *'It's a good job I personally fastened my braces.'*

*

'Prenez garde! I am going to speak in French,' announced Churchill in his speech at the liberation of Paris, *'a formidable undertaking and one which will put great demands upon your friendship for Great Britain.'*

*

Churchill was once playing chess with a friend who was slow to move up his pawns. *'Get out your Baldwins!'* roared Churchill. *'Get out your Baldwins!'*

*

President Roosevelt once remarked after he had entertained Churchill to dinner: *'My dear Winston, the British empire does not exist any longer, it is just a figment of your imagination.'* Churchill rose and walked over to the president, carrying an imaginary load in his arms. *'Do you want India?'* he mischievously asked. Pretending to drop the load into Roosevelt's lap, he added: *'If so, here it is.'*

*

To a barber who asked him how he would like his hair cut: *'A man of my limited resources cannot presume to have a hairstyle. Get on and cut it.'*

*

A personal private secretary to Churchill during World War II recalled the first day she worked for him: **'A paper punch was used to make small holes for the tags in his documents, and during my very first evening with him he astounded me by looking up from the pages of a letter I had just handed him for signature and saying the one word** *"klop"*. **'He was obviously asking me to give him something but I had not the remotest idea what it was. Seeing my bewilderment, he explained that he meant the paper punch.** *"When I say klop, Miss Shearburn, that is what I want."'*

*

February 1951: *'I am informed from many quarters that a rumour has been put about that I died this morning. This is quite untrue.'*

*

In 1931, Churchill was knocked down by a taxi in New York. Recalling the incident later, he commented: *'I do not understand why I was not broken like an eggshell or squashed like a gooseberry.'*

*

The headmaster of Harrow school during Churchill's time there, Rev JEC Welldon, was a stern disciplinarian. He once rebuked the young Winston: **'Churchill, I have very grave reason to be displeased with you.'** The erring student replied: *'And I, sir, have very grave reason to be displeased with you.'*

CHAPTER 13

On Writing, Speaking and Painting

Churchill, in the days when MPs were poorly paid, made his living from writing, while painting provided a welcome release from the pressures and stresses of daily life.

*

'Writing a book is an adventure. To begin with it is a toy and an amusement. Then it becomes a mistress, then it becomes a master, then it becomes a tyrant. The last phase is that just as you are about to be reconciled to your servitude, you kill the monster, and fling him about to the public.'

*

'There is a great deal of difference between the tired man who wants a book to read and the alert man who wants to read a book.'

*

'For my part,' Churchill declared in 1948, *'I consider that it will be found much better by all parties to leave the past to history, especially as I propose to write that history myself.'*

*

Churchill loved books, and wrote of them: *'If you cannot read all your books, at any rate handle, or, as it were, fondle them – peer into them, let them fall open where they will, read from the first sentence that arrests the eye, set them back on their shelves with your own hands, arrange them on your own plan so that if you do not know what is in them, you at least know where they are. Let them be your friends; let them at any rate be your acquaintances.'*

*

In 1899, Churchill discovered that there was another well-known Winston Churchill, who was an American novelist. The two names being the same naturally caused confusion, and the British Winston sent his namesake the following letter: *'Mr Winston Churchill presents his compliments to Mr Winston Churchill, and begs to draw his attention to a matter which concerns them both.*

He has learnt from the press notices that Mr Winston Churchill proposes to bring out another novel entitled Richard Carvel which is certain to have a considerable sale both in England and America.

Mr Winston Churchill is also the author of a novel now being published in serial form in Macmillan's Magazine, and for which he anticipates some sale in both England and America ... He has no doubt that Mr Winston Churchill will recognise from this letter – if indeed by no other means – that there is grave danger of his works being mistaken for those of Mr Winston Churchill. He feels sure that Mr Winston Churchill desires this as little as he does himself.

In future to avoid mistakes as far as possible, Mr Winston Churchill has decided to sign all published articles, stories, or other works "Winston Spencer Churchill", and not "Winston Churchill" as formerly. He trusts that this arrangement will commend itself to Mr Winston Churchill ...

He takes this occasion of complimenting Mr Winston Churchill on the style and success of his works, which are always brought to his notice, whether in magazine or book form, and he trusts that Mr Winston Churchill has derived equal pleasure from any work of his that may have attracted his attention.'

*

Churchill described the development of his own early writing thus: *'I affected a combination of the styles of Macaulay and Gibbon, the staccato antithesis of the former, and the rolling sentences and genitival endings of the latter; and I stuck in a bit of my own from time to time.'*

*

'Broadly speaking, the short words are the best, and the old words, when short, are best of all.'

*

'It is a good thing for an uneducated man to read books of quotations. Bartlett's Familiar Quotations is an admirable work, and I studied it intently. The quotations when engraved upon the memory give you good thoughts.'

*

'There are two things that are more difficult than making an after-dinner speech: climbing a wall which is leaning towards you and kissing a girl who is leaning away from you.'

*

Churchill described the moment he took up painting during World War I: *'And then it was that the muse of painting came to my rescue – out of charity and out of chivalry, because after all she had nothing to do with me – and said: "Are these toys any good for you? They amuse some people ..."'*

*

'When I get to heaven I mean to spend a considerable portion of my first million years in painting, and so get to the bottom of the subject. But then I shall require a still gayer palette than I get here below. I expect orange and vermilion will be the darkest, dullest colours upon it, and beyond them there will be a whole range of wonderful new colours which will delight the celestial eye.'

*

'I cannot pretend to feel impartial about colours. I rejoice with the brilliant ones and am genuinely sorry for the poor browns.'

*

For his paintings of bottles, Churchill coined a new phrase: the bottlescape.

*

A friend once asked Churchill: **'Why do you paint only landscapes?'**

'Because,' replied Winston, *'a tree doesn't complain that I haven't done it justice.'*

*

In 1922, Churchill wrote an article on the joys of painting as a pastime for Strand magazine. *'Every day you may make progress,'* he wrote. *'Every step may be fruitful.*

'Yet there will stretch out before you an ever-lengthening, ever-ascending, ever-improving path. You know that you will never get to the end of the journey. But this, so far from discouraging, only adds to the joy and glory of the climb.'

CHAPTER 14

On Eating, Drinking and Smoking

The Churchill cigar was just as famous as his 'v for victory' sign, and the man was fond of the delights of the table as well as the drinks cabinet.

*

'When I was a young subaltern in the South African war, the water was not fit to drink. To make it palatable we had to put a bit of whisky in it. By diligent effort, I learned to like it.'

*

On a cold day, King George VI asked whether Churchill would care for something to drink to keep out the chill. *'When I was younger I made it a rule never to take strong drink before lunch,'* replied Winston. *'It is now my rule never to do so before breakfast.'*

*

On a rather hasty wartime lunch in the desert:
'No gentleman would eat a ham sandwich without mustard.'

*

Sir Philip Sassoon MP was a very rich man who always entertained his friends and colleagues extremely well. When Churchill was once asked why Sassoon had been given one of his many parliamentary jobs, he replied: *'When you are leaving on a long journey for an unknown destination, it is a good plan to attach a restaurant car at the tail of the train.'*

*

On being presented with a very fine salmon: *'That is indeed a very magnificent fish. I must have some of him. No! No! I will have meat. Carnivores will win this war.'*

*

'Some people say that I have smoked too much. I don't know. If I had not smoked so much, I might have been bad tempered at the wrong time.'

*

'I go by tummy-time and I want my dinner.'

*

Clementine Churchill: **'I hate the taste of beer.'**

Churchill: *'So do most people – to begin with. It is, however, a prejudice that many have been able to overcome.'*

*

'All I can say is that I have taken more out of alcohol than alcohol has taken out of me.'

*

Churchill loved champagne. *'A single glass of champagne imparts a feeling of exhilaration,'* he said. *'The nerves are braced; the imagination is agreeably stirred; the wits become more nimble. A bottle produces a contrary effect. Excess causes a comatose insensibility. So it is with war: and the quality of both is best discovered by sipping.'*

*

Lord Montgomery: **'I neither drink nor smoke and am one hundred per cent fit.'**

Churchill

Churchill: *'I drink and smoke and I am two hundred per cent fit.'*

*

Although he was often accused of being under the influence, Churchill made clear his views in 1930: *'I had been brought up and trained to have the utmost contempt for people who got drunk – and I would have liked to have the boozing scholars of the universities wheeled into line and properly chastised for their squalid misuse of what I must ever regard as a gift of the gods.'*

*

'My rule of life prescribed as an absolutely sacred rite smoking cigars and also the drinking of alcohol before, after and if need be during all meals and in the intervals between them.'

Acknowledgements

The following publications, authors and publishers
are gratefully acknowledged:

FE, by the Earl of Birkenhead (Eyre & Spottiswoode)

Churchill by his contemporaries, ed Charles Eade
(Hutchinson)

Second World War, by WS Churchill (Cassell)

The war and Colonel Warden, by Gerard Pawle
(Harrap)

My years with Churchill, by Norman McGowan
(Souvenir Press)

The memoirs of Lord Ismay (Heinemann)

My early life, by WS Churchill (Thornton
Butterworth)

Thoughts and adventures, by WS Churchill (Thornton
Butterworth)

Turn of the tide, by Sir A Bryant (Collins)

Triumph in the west, by Sir A Bryant (Collins)

The prof in two worlds, by the Earl of Birkenhead (Collins)

The wit of Sir Winston, compiled Adam Sykes and Iain Sproat (Leslie Frewin)

War speeches, compiled by Charles Eade (Cassell)

My yesterday, your tomorrow, by Lord Boothby (Hutchinson)

Politicians and the war, by Lord Beaverbrook (Oldbourne)

As it happened, by Lord Attlee (Heinemann)

Great contemporaries, by WS Churchill (Thornton Butterworth)

The finest hours, by Jack Le Vien (Corgi)

The valiant years, by Jack Le Vien (Corgi)

New statesmanship, an anthology, ed Edward Hyams (Longmans)

Acknowledgements

The wit of Winston Churchill, by Geoffrey Williams and Charles Roetter (Max Parrish)

Nine troubled years, by Lord Templewood (Collins)

Mr Churchill in 1940, by Isaiah Berlin (John Murray)

The call to honour, by Charles de Gaulle (Collins)

Old men forget, by Duff Cooper (Rupert Hart-Davies)

Edward Marsh, a biography, by Christopher Hassall (Longmans)

The Baldwin age, edited by John Raymond (Eyre & Spottiswoode)

Headlines all my life, by Arthur Christiansen (Heinemann)

The Yankee Marlborough, by R W Thompson (George Allen & Unwin)

Unity, by Charles de Gaulle (Weidenfeld & Nicolson)

Five lives, by the Earl of Longford (Hutchinson)

The age of Churchill, by Peter de Mendelssohn (Thames & Hudson)

Churchill

Churchill the great, ed Victor Sim (Mirror
Newspapers)

My darling Clementine, by Jack Fishman (WH Allen)

Churchill's art of government, by Viscount Eccles
(The Sunday Times)

Randolph Churchill Remembers (The Sunday Times)

Hansard

The British Broadcasting Corporation